Sometimes We Feel Sad

By Reggie Harper

Cavendish Square

New York

Published in 2022 by Cavendish Square Publishing, LLC
243 5th Avenue, Suite 136, New York, NY 10016

Copyright © 2022 by Cavendish Square Publishing, LLC

First Edition

Website: cavendishsq.com

This publication represents the opinions and views of the author based on his or her personal experience, knowledge, and research. The information in this book serves as a general guide only. The author and publisher have used their best efforts in preparing this book and disclaim liability rising directly or indirectly from the use and application of this book.

All websites were available and accurate when this book was sent to press.

Library of Congress Cataloging-in-Publication Data

Names: Harper, Reggie, author.
Title: Sometimes we feel sad / Reggie Harper.
Description: New York : Cavendish Square Publishing, [2022] | Series: Dealing with your feelings | Includes index.
Identifiers: LCCN 2020030636 | ISBN 9781502659804 (library binding) | ISBN 9781502659781 (paperback) | ISBN 9781502659798 (set) | ISBN 9781502659811 (ebook)
Subjects: LCSH: Sadness in children–Juvenile literature. | Sadness–Juvenile literature.
Classification: LCC BF723.S15 K44 2022 | DDC 155.4/124–dc23
LC record available at https://lccn.loc.gov/2020030636

Editor: Caitie McAneney
Designer: Deanna Paternostro

The photographs in this book are used by permission and through the courtesy of: Cover Monkey Business Images/Shutterstock.com; p. 5 Justin Paget/DigitalVision/Getty Images; p. 7 omgimages/iStock/Getty Images Plus/Getty Images; p. 9 LWA/Stone/Getty Images; p. 11 skynesher/E+/Getty Images; p. 13 Halfpoint Images/Moment/Getty Images; p. 15 Jose Luis Pelaez Inc/DigitalVision/Getty Images; p. 17 Annie Otzen/Moment/Getty Images; p. 19 fStop Images - Alejandro Nino/Brand X Pictures/Getty Images; p. 21 MoMo Productions/DigitalVision/Getty Images; p. 23 Cavan Images/Cavan/Getty Images.

Some of the images in this book illustrate individuals who are models. The depictions do not imply actual situations or events.

CPSIA compliance information: Batch #CS22CSQ: For further information contact Cavendish Square Publishing LLC, New York, New York, at 1-877-980-4450.

Printed in the United States of America

Find us on

CONTENTS

Feeling Sad

Do you ever feel down?
Do you ever want to cry?
This feeling is called sadness.
You might feel sad for a small
reason or for a big reason. It's
normal to feel sad sometimes.

Sometimes we are sad for a short time. Maybe you lost your **favorite** toy. Maybe you can't play outside because it's raining. These things can make you feel down. It's OK to feel sad about small things.

Sometimes we are sad for a big reason. Maybe your friend moved away. Maybe someone was mean to you. You might feel sad for a little longer. You might need help to feel better.

Big Feelings

What does it feel like to be sad? You might frown. You might want to cry. You might find it hard to feel **calm**. You might find it hard to **focus** at school.

It can be hard to do
fun things when you're sad.
It can be hard to smile.
You might feel like staying
home. You might feel like
you need a hug.

Sadness can be a big feeling. It might bring thoughts about how bad things seem or feel. It's normal to feel this way sometimes. Things won't feel bad forever.

Dealing with Sadness

Sometimes we cry when we are sad. We don't want to talk to friends. We don't want to do fun things. We think sad thoughts over and over. We don't tell people how we feel.

You can use tools to deal with sadness. You can notice your sadness. You can tell yourself it's OK. It will pass. You can believe in yourself. You are more than your sad feelings.

Other people can help! You
can talk to friends. You can
talk to family. You can talk
to your teacher. They will
understand. It feels good to
talk about why you are sad.

21

What makes you happy?
You can still do those things if
you are sad. Sometimes, they
can help you feel better. You
can go for a walk. You can
listen to music. You can play.
Soon, you will feel better!

WORDS TO KNOW

calm: A feeling of peace.

favorite: Liked best.

focus: To direct attention at something.

normal: Usual.

INDEX

24